DK Get Talking

CHINESE

Workbook

Mandarin Chinese
practice for beginners

Author Elinor Greenwood
Consultant Katharine Carruthers
US Editor Allison Singer
Art Editors Emma Hobson, Hoa Luc
Editor Cecile Landau
Art Director Martin Wilson
Publishing Manager Bridget Giles
Producer, pre-production Francesca Wardell
Producer Christine Ni

First American Edition, 2015
Published in the United States by DK Publishing
345 Hudson Street, New York, New York 10014

A catalog record for this book is available from the
Library of Congress.
ISBN 978-1-4654-3588-0

DK books are available at special discounts when
purchased in bulk for sales promotions, premiums,
fund-raising, or educational use. For details,
contact: DK Publishing Special
Markets, 345 Hudson Street, New York,
New York 10014
SpecialSales@dk.com

Printed and bound in China

Contents

加油!
Jiā yóu!
Go for it!

Foreword

This is a workbook, and learning Chinese is the mission. Here are five tips to help.

1 Take the chance to practice when you can.

你好
Nǐ hǎo!

2 Go slow. Half an hour a day is better than two straight hours.

3 Test yourself. Make flash cards and doodle characters in spare moments.

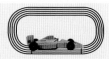
文

4 Check your work; repeat, repeat, and make sure it's all gone in.

5 Practice makes perfect, so using this workbook is a great start.

太好了!
Fantastic!

Top ten most common Chinese characters

These are all in the book.

1 de — possessive particle — 的

6 rén — person — 人

2 yī — one — 一

7 wǒ — I — 我

3 shì — to be — 是

8 zài — at — 在

4 bù — no/not — 不

9 yǒu — to have — 有

5 le — verb particle — 了

10 tā — he — 他

A companion book

This workbook is a companion book to *Get Talking Chinese* (available wherever books are sold). All the pronunciations are available on the CD attached to that book.

Using the workbook

Although this is a "work" book, it's fun, too! There is space to doodle and draw as well as other fun activities. Featured inside:

- Memory tips and pinyin practice
- How to write all the characters with clear stroke order
- Key characters that you won't forget
- Grid paper at the end of each section to help you practice what you've learned
- Pronunciation tips

Keeping it simple

This book includes useful and commonly used Chinese characters. The information is not overwhelming, with a pace of roughly six characters per double-page spread.

Remember, the secret to learning Chinese is:

 Màn màn lái!
Take it easy!

Pinyin and tones

Chinese has no alphabet. The written language is made up of Chinese characters. These characters give no clue to pronunciation, so a pronunciation system has developed in roman letters. This system is called pinyin.
For example, 中文 is written **Zhōngwén** in pinyin.

Tones and tone marks

Mandarin Chinese has four tones, and one "toneless" tone. The tone you use when pronouncing each one-syllable sound determines the meaning. The tone marks ˉ ´ ˇ ˋ on the vowel show which tone to use.

Here is how to pronounce the different tones:

1ˢᵗ tone high level

Pitch your voice high and hold the sound there slightly longer than seems natural.

mā
mother

As a doctor tells you when looking down your throat. Say:

Aaah!

2ⁿᵈ tone rising

From the middle level of your voice range to the top. Raise your eyebrows as you say it!

má
hemp

Like the tone at the end of a question.

What?

Numbering the tones

The tones are numbered, and when you are learning Chinese, it is good to know which tone is which number.

Practice by writing the tone marks on these pinyin words:

3rd tone:	mi	4th tone:	mi	1st tone:	mi
1st tone:	zhu	2nd tone:	zhu	3rd tone:	zhu
4th tone:	ba	1st tone:	ba	2nd tone:	ba

3rd tone   falling then rising

From the middle level, down deep, then up a bit.

mǎ

horse

Like when you're surprised.

Really?

4th tone   falling

A short, sharp fall from your high voice pitch. Stamp your foot as you say it!

mà

scold

The tone of a statement.

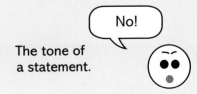

No!

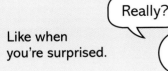

Different strokes

Chinese characters are not random squiggles. They are made up of set strokes.

Copy these strokes in the boxes provided. Follow the direction of the arrows.

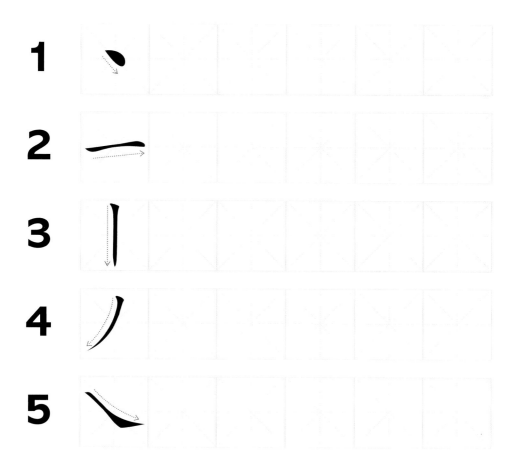

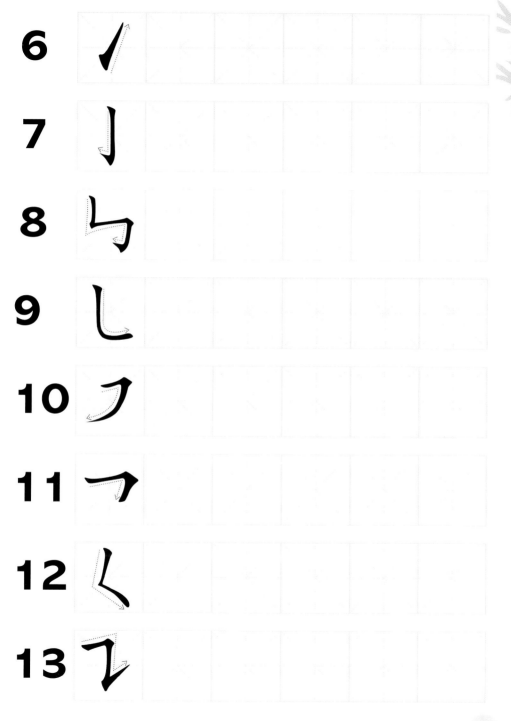

Stroke order

The characters are arranged in a set way, too. Follow the
correct stroke order to write beautiful characters.

**Follow the numbered strokes to write the characters.
The two general rules are:**

1 Write top to bottom

三
sān
three

Trace   Freehand

2 And left to right

川
chuān
river

**Practice writing these characters using the above
two rules.**

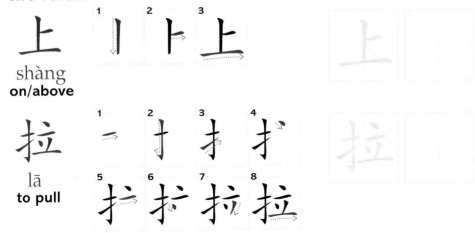

上
shàng
on/above

拉
lā
to pull

Common variations

There are variations, however. It depended on what made fewer splotches when scholars used brushes and ink to write.

Here are some examples.

Horizontal before vertical

十
shí
ten

Outside then inside

月
yuè
moon

Center before outside

小
xiǎo
small

Left vertical first

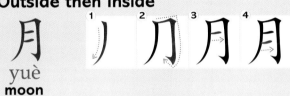

口
kǒu
mouth

Bottom horizontal last

王
wāng
king

Mixing it up

In any block of Chinese text, these different stroke orders are represented.

Try writing the characters in the boxes using the correct stroke order, then check your work afterward.

First cover up the right side of the dotted line. No peeking!

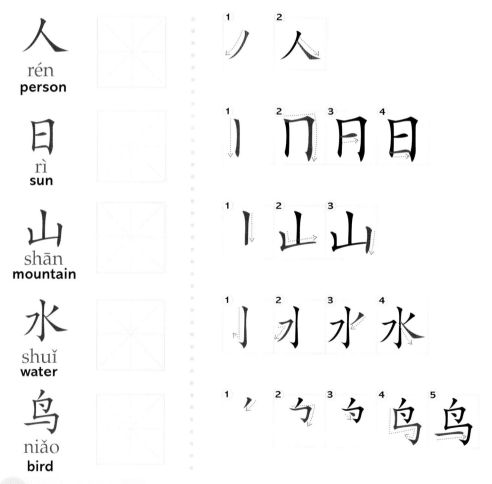

人
rén
person

日
rì
sun

山
shān
mountain

水
shuǐ
water

鸟
niǎo
bird

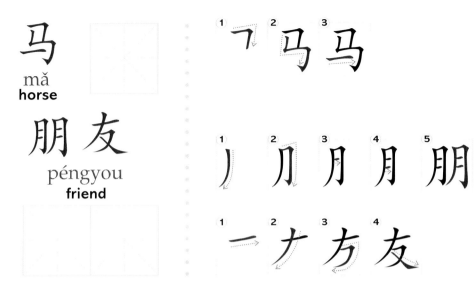

Did you get the stroke order right? If you did, good job! But don't worry if you didn't. This is an aspect of learning Chinese that will eventually become second nature—especially if you concentrate on following the stroke orders in this book.

Picture it!

The original characters, written more than 2,000 years ago, were pictures of things. Some Chinese characters to this day are pictographs. Drawing on characters (whether they are pictographs or not) is a good way to help you to remember them.

Draw on these characters. *Look at the example.*

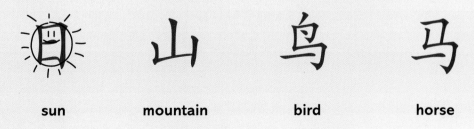

| sun | mountain | bird | horse |

It's radical

Some characters can be found making up parts of other characters. These characters then become "radicals." There are 214 radicals in total, and they can give clues to meaning and pronunciation.

To start, practice writing these four characters:

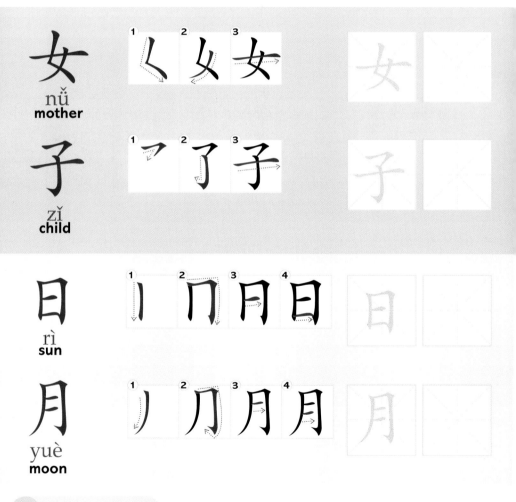

女
nǚ
mother

子
zǐ
child

日
rì
sun

月
yuè
moon

Notice how the meanings of the new characters directly relate to the meanings of the original characters.

Like building blocks, you put the characters together to make new ones.

好
hǎo
good

(literally mother and child together)

明
míng
bright

(literally sun and moon together)

Character practice 1

Practice writing the characters from this section here.

2 Let's get started
First words

These are among the first words to learn in any language.

nǐ hǎo
hello

Copy the pinyin here:

....

How to write it:

Your turn:

xièxie

thank you

zàijiàn

good-bye

Your turn:

Your turn:

Fill in the speech bubbles. What's the person saying?
Answers in the back.

How are you?

Asking "How are you?" is a good way to greet people in China, too.

First of all, learn these pronouns.

wǒ

I

How to write it:

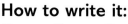

Your turn:

nǐ

you

How to write it:

Your turn:

Hello + "ma"

To say "How are you?" simply add "ma" to nǐ hǎo.

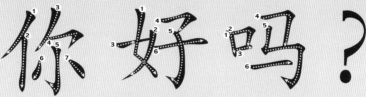

Nǐ hǎo ma?

How are you?

Your turn:

你 好 吗 ？

Copy the pinyin here:

....

I'm very well

Now answer the question.

我 很 好

Wǒ hěn hǎo.

I'm very well.

Your turn:

Copy the
pinyin here:

....

....

Where is it?

Being able to ask where things are will help you find your way in China.

First learn these key characters.

在哪儿？

zài nǎr...?
where is...?

Copy the pinyin here:

....

How to write it:

Your turn:

Now ask the way

To ask where something is, you simply add "zài nǎr?" to the word for what you are looking for. Here is an example: **Fàndiàn** means restaurant. **Fàndiàn zài nǎr?** means "Where's the restaurant?" (Translated literally, this means "Restaurant at where?")

Ask where each of these places are, using pinyin. Remember to put the noun first! *Answers in the back.*

1

饭店
fàndiàn
restaurant

Where is the restaurant?

....

2

书店
shūdiàn
bookstore

Where is the bookstore?

....

3

茶馆
cháguǎn
teahouse

Where is the teahouse?

....

4

厕所
cèsuǒ
restroom

Where are the restrooms?

....

Ladies and gents

The characters for "man" and "woman" are good to know, especially because they are the bathroom signs in China.

nǚ
woman

Picture it

Draw a head, hands, and shoes on the character to help you remember it.

 The pinyin for "nü" has two dots above the "u" indicating a round "ooo" sound.

How to write it:

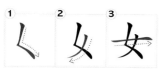

Your turn:

Three characters for the price of one

The character for "man" is made up of two other characters:

田	+	力	=	男
tián		lì		nán
field		**strength**		**man**

Together they literally mean "strength in the field." When the character was invented more than 2,000 years ago, most men worked in paddy fields.

nán
man

Memory tip!
Change the "m" in "man" to an "n" and you get "nan"!

How to write it:

Your turn:

Welcome!

Give a warm welcome by inviting someone in for a nice cup of tea.

qǐng
please
(pronounced "ching")

How to write it:

1. ゝ
2. ネ
3. ネー
4. ネラ
5. ネ
6. ネー
7. 请
8. 请
9. 请
10. 请

Your turn:

请 ☐ ☐

Fill in the spaces with one (or two) of these characters in the boxes.
Answers in the back.

进 喝茶 坐

1 Please come in!

Your turn:

请 ☐

jìn
to enter

Your turn:

zuò
to sit

Your turn:

hē
to drink

Your turn:

chá
tea

Your turn:

2

Please sit down!

Your turn:

3

Please have a cup of tea.

Your turn:

What's your name?

Learn how to reply when someone asks you what your name is.

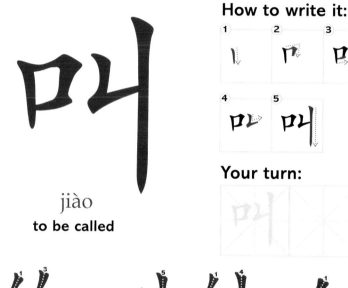

How to write it:

jiào

to be called

Your turn:

Nǐ jiào shénme?

What's your name?

Your turn:

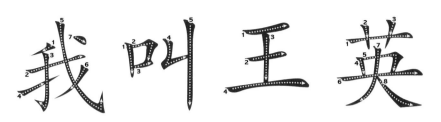

Wǒ jiào Wáng Yīng.

I'm called Wang Ying.

Wang is a common last name. Note: Last names come first in China.

Ying is a common first name and means "brave."

Your turn:

Answer the question using pinyin and your own name.

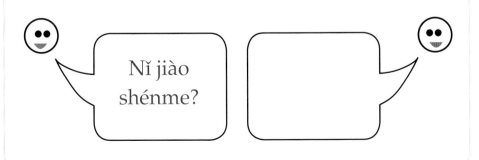

Nǐ jiào shénme?

Character practice 2

Practice the characters from this section here.

在 哪 儿 ？

饭 店

书 店

茶 馆

厕 所

女

男

请

More to do!

Keep going. This section includes these characters, too.

Practice squares

Extra space for extra practice.

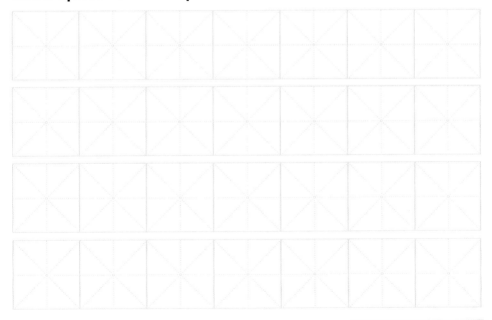

Head...

These next pages include body vocabulary, starting at the top.

tóu
head

tóufa
hair

ěrduo
ear

yǎnjing
eye

鼻子

bízi

nose

嘴巴

zuǐba

mouth

Label the girl's head with the correct characters, or pinyin...or both! Whichever you prefer.

...to tail

Copy the Chinese characters for the parts of the body.

dùzi
stomach

gēbo
arm

shǒu
hand

tuǐ
leg

脚
jiǎo
foot

脚 ⎯ 脚

Label the lady.

Sizing things up

Here are two really easy characters to learn: big and small.

dà
big

Picture it

The character for "big" looks like a man with outstretched arms. Draw on hands and a head.

How to write it:

Your turn:

Copy the pinyin here:

....

Big or small?

Write whether the objects are big or small in Chinese characters. *Answers in the back.*

1

2

Itty bitty things

With Chinese characters, small details matter. For example: 小
Take note of the little dots on each side, and the little flick up to
the left on the down stroke.

Remember, all Chinese characters take up the same amount of space on the paper and there is an equal distance between each one.

学习中文很有意思。中文的字很漂亮。我喜欢学习中文。你呢？

xiǎo
small
(pronounced "sh-yaow")

How to write it:

1   2   3

Your turn:

Copy the pinyin here:

....

3

4

De-der!

This character is the number one most common character in Chinese. Its meaning isn't too glamorous. It's the possessive particle.

de
[**possessive particle**]

How to write it:

1 2 3 4 5 6 7 8
ノ 亻 亻 白 白 白 的 的

Your turn:

的   的   的

"De" can be added to just about anything as a connector. It shows possession. For example, in English, an apostrophe "s" is used: "The ship's cat" means "the cat that belongs to the ship." In Chinese, "de" is used, so you would say, "ship **de** cat." That is why it is so common.

"I" into "my"

Here "de" is used to make "I" into "my," and "you" into "your."

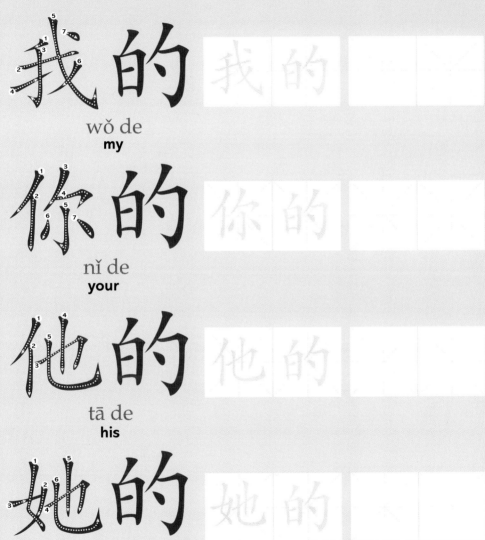

我 的
wǒ de
my

你 的
nǐ de
your

他 的
tā de
his

她 的
tā de
her

"Tā de" (his) and "tā de" (her) differ only in the characters. Notice the woman radical making the difference.

Family and friends

There are two words for "brother" and two for "sister" depending on whether older or younger.

māma
mother

bàba
father

mèimei
younger sister

jiějie
older sister

dìdi
younger brother

gēge
older brother

Making introductions

Knowing how to introduce someone is polite and useful.

Your turn:

zhè shì
this is

Put these words together to introduce a family member.

For example:

Zhè shì + wǒ de + mèimei.

= **This is** **my** **younger sister.**

Write "This is my mother" in pinyin here:

Answer in the back.

Character practice 3

Practice writing the characters from this section here.

脚
手
腿
大
小
的
我 的
你 的
他 的

More to do!

Keep going. This section includes these characters, too.

她 的

妈 妈

爸 爸

妹 妹

姐 姐

弟 弟

哥 哥

这 是

Practice squares

Extra space for extra practice.

4 Countries

The Middle Kingdom

In ancient times, the regions around China paid tribute to the Chinese Emperor, and China came to be called the Middle Kingdom.

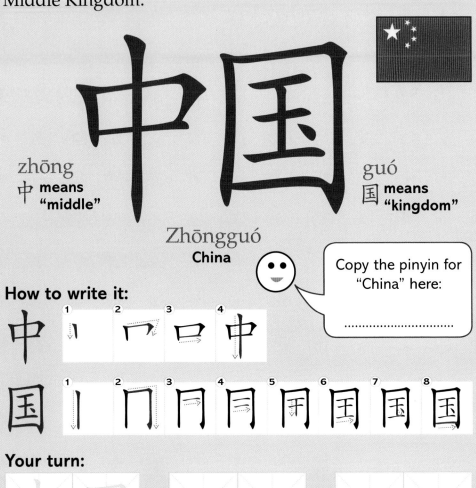

zhōng
中 means "middle"

guó
国 means "kingdom"

Zhōngguó
China

Copy the pinyin for "China" here:

....

How to write it:

Your turn:

A character with legs

The character for "person" is an ancient pictogram and looks like two legs walking.

How to write it:

rén
person

Picture it! Draw a head and feet on the character to help you remember it.

Your turn:

Just add "rén" to "Zhōngguó" to say "Chinese person."

中 国 人

Zhōngguórén
Chinese person

Your turn:

Countries of the world

In Chinese, the names of other countries are translated using characters with the appropriate sound. Or they can be literal translations, in the case of Japan.

Translating the characters gives interesting, and flattering, results. Some country names are purely phonetic, however, as with "Holland" (The Netherlands).

Měiguó USA ("beautiful country")

Yīngguó Britain ("brave country")

Fǎguó France ("legal country")

Déguó Germany ("virtuous country")

Rìběn Japan ("rising sun")

Hélán Netherlands (phonetic "Holland")

Jiānádà Canada (phonetic)

Where are you from?

This is the question strangers in China will ask you before any other.

nǎ
which

How to write it:

1	2	3	4	5
丨	冂	口	叮	叮

6	7	8	9
叼	叨	哪	哪

Your turn:

哪

Copy the question and answer in the boxes provided.

你 是 哪 国 人？

Nǐ shì nǎ guó rén?   **Which country are you from?**

我 是 美 国 人

Wǒ shì Měiguórén.   **I am American.**

Geography test

Look back a page at the countries' names, then try labeling the globe using pinyin. *Answers in the back.*

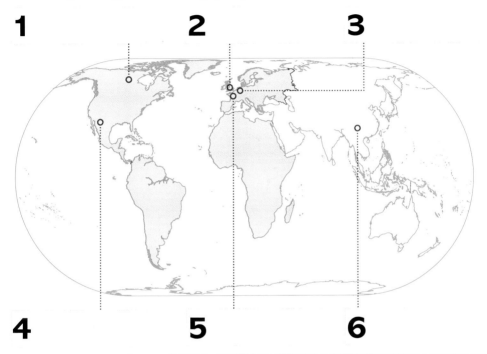

1　　　　　　**2**　　　　　　**3**

4　　　　　　**5**　　　　　　**6**

Your turn

Translate from English into pinyin.
Answers in the back.

Remember, by adding "rén" to the country's name you are saying "people" of that country.

1 Where are you from? ....

2 I am American. ....

3 I am French. ....

4 I am Japanese. ....

Character practice 4

Practice writing the characters from this section here.

Practice squares

Extra space for extra practice.

Numbers 1–10

Learning numbers 1–10 is simple and very useful. The characters for numbers 1–3 are the easiest of them all.

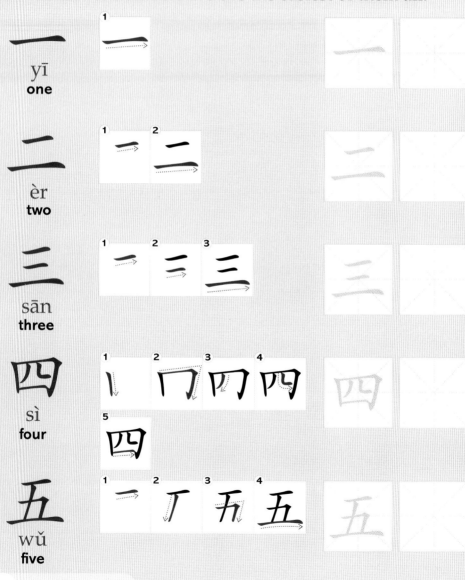

yī
one

èr
two

sān
three

sì
four

wǔ
five

六
liù
six

1 `丶` 2 `二` 3 `亠` 4 六

七
qī
seven

1 `一` 2 七

八
bā
eight

1 `丿` 2 八

九
jiǔ
nine

1 `丿` 2 九

十
shí
ten

1 `一` 2 十

10 to a million

To count above 10, it takes some simple math.

- If a number comes **after** 10 (十), you **add** it to 10.
- If a number comes **before** 10 (十), you **times** it by 10.

How it works...

十三	shísān	13	3 **after** 10 so that means 10 + 3
三十	sānshí	30	3 **before** 10 so that means 3 x 10
三十二	sānshíèr	32	2 **after** and 3 **before** 10 so that means (3 x 10) + 2

What are these numbers? *Answers in the back.*

1 十五

5 二十三

2 四十

6 七十一

3 十八

7 九十九

4 十四

8 五十八

100 +

Higher numbers string together in the same way, with 10, 100, 1,000, and so on acting as "stops." Practice writing the number words, then try the math test below.

bǎi
100

qiān
1,000

wàn
10,000

百   千   万

Look at these numbers as an example:

四百三十	sìbǎisānshí	430
三千二百	sānqiānèrbǎi	3,200
五万	wǔwàn	50,000

Math test
Do you know what these numbers are? *Answers in the back.*

(1) 二百三十

(2) 六万

(3) 四千三百

(4) 九万

Days of the week

Here numbers 1–6 count out the days of the week.

xīngqī

weekday
(pronounce this "shingchee")

How to write it:

星　1 ⟍　2 ⊓　3 ⊓　4 日　5 尸　6 旦　7 旦　8 星

9 星

期　1 ⟋　2 ⼗　3 卄　4 廿　5 甘　6 其　7 其　8 其

9 其　10 期　11 期　12 期

Your turn:

Once you can write "weekday" in Chinese, you add the numbers 1–6 to get Monday (literally "weekday 1") to Saturday ("weekday 6"). Only Sunday is different.

Monday xīngqīyī	星	期	一			
Tuesday xīngqīèr	星	期	二			
Wednesday xīngqīsān	星	期	三			
Thursday xīngqīsì	星	期	四			
Friday xīngqīwǔ	星	期	五			
Saturday xīngqīliù	星	期	六			
Sunday xīngqītiān	星	期	天			

Months of the year

Once you've learned the basic numbers, it's really easy to also learn the months of the year.

First learn this character, which is a pictograph of the moon.

yuè

moon/month

Copy the pinyin here:

....

Picture it
Draw on the character and turn it into a crescent moon.

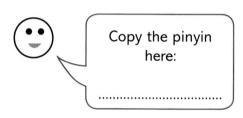

How to write it:

Your turn:

January
一月

yīyuè

February
二月

èryuè

March
三月

sānyuè

April
四月

sìyuè

May
五月

wǔyuè

June
六月

liùyuè

July
七月

qīyuè

August
八月

bāyuè

September
九月

jiǔyuè

October
十月

shíyuè

November
十一月

shíyīyuè

December
十二月

shíèryuè

Birthday party

People in China are likely to celebrate their birthdays with a cake and by singing "Happy Birthday" (in Mandarin, of course).

生 日 快 乐!

Shēngrì kuàilè!

Happy birthday!

How to write it:

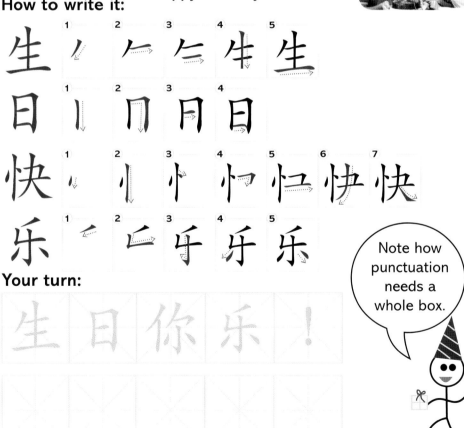

Your turn:

Note how punctuation needs a whole box.

How old are you?

There are two ways to ask this question in Chinese. The first is for adults and older children:

Nǐ duō dà?

How old are you?

Your turn:

你 多 大 ？

The second is for children under ten:

你几岁？

Nǐ jǐ suì?

How old are you?

Answer the question using your number knowledge by inserting your age in the space provided.

我 ············· 岁

Wǒ ············· suì.

I'm ············ years old.

Character practice 5

Practice writing the characters from this section here.

九

十

百

千

万

星期一

星期二

星期三

星期四

More to do!

Keep going. This section includes these characters, too.

六月
七月
八月
九月
十月
十一月
十二月
生日你乐！

North to south

China is big, and major cities experience different weather.

北

běi

north

How to write it:

Your turn:

Beijing (literally meaning "northern capital") is in north China. It's hot in the summer, and below freezing in winter.

东

dōng

east

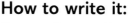

How to write it:

Your turn:

Shanghai is in the east. It has a warm spring, a hot, rainy summer, a cool autumn, and a cold winter.

南

nán

south

How to write it:

Your turn:

Guangzhou (Canton) is in the south. It has warm winters and hot, humid summers.

西

xī

west

How to write it:

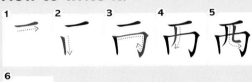

Your turn:

Chengdu is in the west. It's warm in spring, sultry in summer, and rainy in autumn. The winter is cold.

Seasons

The seasons in China vary depending on where you are.

First learn the character common to them all, then practice writing the seasons in the boxes.

tiān

day/heaven

Picture it

See how the character has formed:

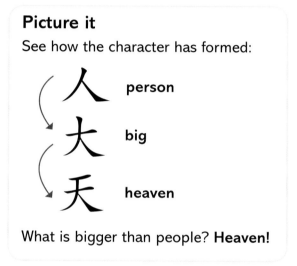

人 **person**

大 **big**

天 **heaven**

What is bigger than people? **Heaven!**

How to write it:

1　2　3　4

🙂 Copy the pinyin here:

·····························

Your turn:

春天

chūntiān **spring**

夏天

xiàtiān **summer**

秋天

qiūtiān **autumn**

冬天

dōngtiān **winter**

Weather words

Find out the weather forecast… in Chinese.

热

rè

hot

How to write it:

Your turn:

冷

lěng

cold

How to write it:

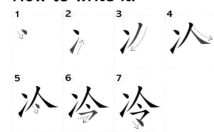

Your turn:

下雨

xià yǔ

rainy

(pronounced "shar yoo")

How to write it:

下 ¹一 ²丁 ³下

雨 ¹一 ²冂 ³冇 ⁴帀

⁵帀 ⁶雨 ⁷雨 ⁸雨

刮风

guā fēng

windy

(pronounced "guh-wah fung")

How to write it:

刮 ¹丿 ²二 ³千 ⁴千

⁵舌 ⁶舌 ⁷刮 ⁸刮

风 ¹丿 ²几 ³风 ⁴风

Your turn:

下 雨

Your turn:

刮 风

Character practice 6

Practice writing the characters from this section here.

Practice squares

Extra space for extra practice.

Traffic report

Knowing the words for "car," "bus," and "train" is useful for traveling on China's public transportation system.

First learn this character:

ché
vehicle
(pronounced "ch-uh")

Copy the pinyin here:

....

Picture it

This character was originally a pictograph of a horse-drawn cart (as seen from above).

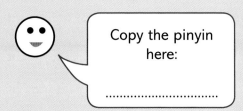

重 seal script

車 old style character

车 new character used in China today

How to write it:

Your turn:

Traffic jam

飞机

fēijī
airplane

All these modes of transportation have "che" meaning "vehicle" at the end. "Airplane" is the exception. ("Feiji" literally means "flying machine.")

Your turn:

zìxíngchē
bicycle
(pronounced "z-uh shing ch-uh")

火车

Your turn:

huǒchē
train

汽车

Your turn:

qìchē
car

出租车
chūzūchē
taxi

beep!

公共汽车
gōnggòngqìchē
bus

Finding the way

Make being lost in China a thing of the past with these useful words.

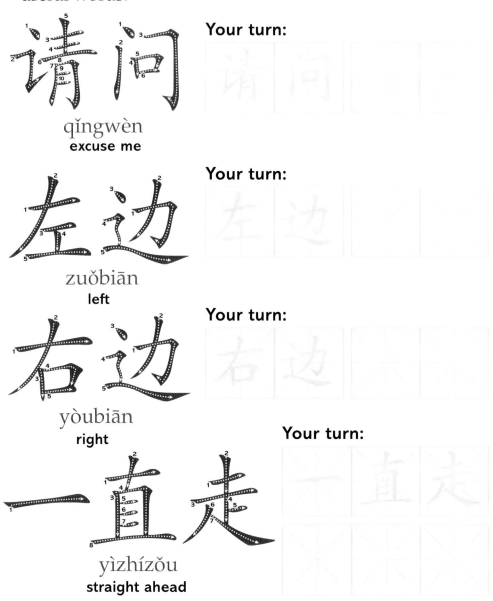

Your turn:

qǐngwèn
excuse me

Your turn:

zuǒbiān
left

Your turn:

yòubiān
right

Your turn:

yìzhízǒu
straight ahead

Give directions

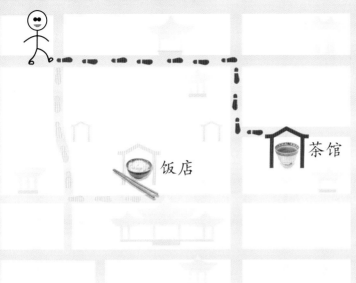

饭店

茶馆

Try giving directions to the lost tourist. Number the directions in the right order. *Answers at the back.*

1 请问。饭店在哪儿?

Qǐngwèn. Fàndiàn zài nǎr?

Excuse me. Where is the restaurant?

yòubiān　　　　　yìzhízǒu　　　　　zuǒbiān

2 请问。茶馆在哪儿?

Qǐngwèn. Cháguǎn zài nǎr?

Excuse me. Where is the tea shop?

zuǒbiān　　　　　yòubiān　　　　　yìzhízǒu

Telling the time

If you are going somewhere, you will need to know what time your bus or train is leaving.

Follow these three rules:

1 Add **"diǎn"** to a number to say **"o'clock."** For example, **"sān diǎn"** is **"three o'clock."**

2 Add **"diǎn bàn"** to say **"half past."** For example, **"sān diǎn bàn"** is **"half past three."**

3 Add however many **"fēn"** (minutes) to make other times. For example, **"sān diǎn èrshí fēn"** is **"3:20"**—literally **"3 o'clock, 20 minutes."**

Practice the new characters first.

Your turn:

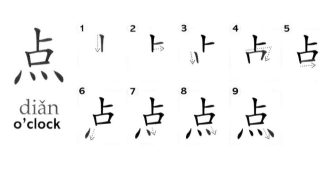

diǎn
o'clock

Your turn:

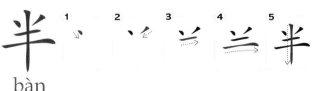

bàn
half

分

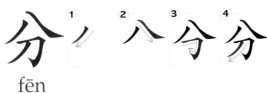

fēn
minute

Now try to tell the time on the clocks. Follow the example. *Answers at the back.*

1

sān diǎn bàn

2

3

4

Buying a ticket

Asking to buy a ticket is the final step.

I want to buy a ticket to Beijing.

Here's how to ask:

我想买票。去北京

Wǒ xiǎng mǎi piào. Qù Běijīng.

Here is the vocabulary broken down. Practice each word individually in the boxes.

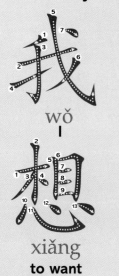

wǒ
I

xiǎng
to want

mǎi
to buy

Your turn:

Your turn:

Your turn:

piào
ticket

Your turn:

qù
to go

Your turn:

Běijīng
Beijing

Your turn:

Now put the words together. (Note there are two sentences in the Chinese.)

Here are the simple answers you can expect to hear.

没有 Méi yǒu.

I don't have one.
(pronounced "may yo")

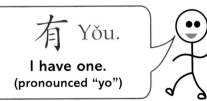

有 Yǒu.

I have one.
(pronounced "yo")

Character practice 7

Practice the characters from this section here.

点

半

分

我

想

买

票

去

北京

Chopsticks and bowl

When in China, eating with chopsticks is the norm.

kuàizi

chopsticks

How to write it:

筷

子

Your turn:

碗

Your turn:

wǎn
bowl

勺子

Your turn:

sháozi
spoon

刀

Your turn:

dāo
knife

叉

Your turn:

chā
fork

Table talk

Impress people at your next Chinese meal by knowing some useful foodie phrases.

很好吃！

Hěn hǎo chī!

It's delicious!

Your turn:

很 好 吃 ！

Copy the pinyin here:

....

....

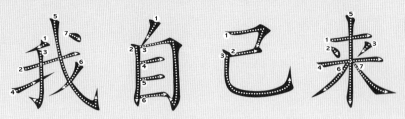

Wǒ zìjǐ lái.

I'll help myself.

Your turn:

Copy the
pinyin here:

....

....

Wǒ chī bǎo le.

I'm full.

Your turn:

Copy the
pinyin here:

....

....

Reading a menu

Look at the menu and choose a delicious dish.

Copy the characters.

Your turn:

米饭
mǐfàn
rice

Your turn:

面条
miàntiáo
noodles

Your turn:

蔬菜
shūcài
vegetables

yú

fish

Your turn:

jī

chicken

Your turn:

shuǐguǒ

fruit

Your turn:

diǎnxīn

dim sum

Your turn:

Restaurant words

You've chosen what you want to eat. Now you need to communicate with the waiter.

fúwùyuán

waiter/waitress

Your turn:

càidān

menu

Your turn:

fàndiàn

restaurant

Your turn:

măidān

bill

Your turn:

买 单 买 单

chī

to eat

Your turn:

吃 吃

xiăng

to want

Your turn:

想 想

Look at the speech bubble. Can you guess what he is saying? *Answer in the back.*

"Fúwùyuán, wǒ xiǎng chī diǎnxīn."

....

....

Character practice 8

Practice the characters from this section here.

筷子
碗
勺子
刀
叉
很好吃
我自己来

我 吃 饱 了

米 饭

面 条

蔬 菜

鱼

鸡

水 果

点 心

More to do!

Keep going. This section includes these characters, too.

服 务 员

菜 单

饭 店

买 单

吃

想

Practice squares

Extra space for extra practice!

9 Fun and games

Hobbies

As well as learning Chinese, you may have other hobbies.

huàhuà
painting

Your turn:

tīng yīnyuè
listening to music

Your turn:

看书

kàn shū

reading
(pronounced "kan shoo")

Your turn:

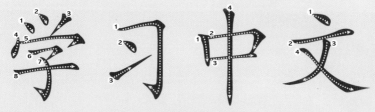

学习中文

xuéxí Zhōngwén

learning Chinese
(pronounced "shoo-ay-shee jong-wen")

Your turn:

Ball games

Sports are important in China, with soccer and basketball being the most popular.

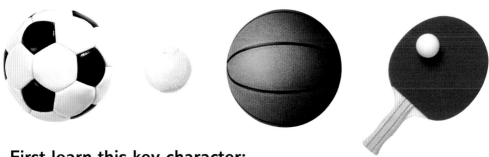

First learn this key character:

qiú

ball
(pronounced "chee-oo")

How to write it:

Copy the pinyin here:

....

Your turn:

wǎngqiú

tennis

Your turn:

zúqiú

soccer

Your turn:

lánqiú

basketball

Your turn:

pīngpāngqiú

table tennis

Your turn:

Like it/love it

Learn how to say "I love you" in Chinese.

ài
to love
(pronounced "I")

How to write it:

Copy the pinyin here:

....

Your turn:

我 爱 你
Wǒ ài nǐ.
I love you.
(pronounced "war I knee")

Saying "boo"

Now learn how to say you like, or don't like, things.

First practice writing these characters:

Your turn:

xǐhuan
to like
(pronounced "shee-hoo-an")

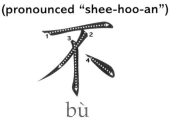

Your turn:

bù
not/no
(pronounced "boo")

To say you like a sport, you say:

我 喜 欢 乒 乓 球

Wǒ **xǐhuan** pīngpāngqiú.
I like table tennis

To say you "don't like" something, you add "bù" in front of the verb:

我 不 喜 欢 网 球

Wǒ **bù xǐhuan** wǎngqiú.
I don't like tennis.

Character practice 9

Practice the characters from this section here.

Practice squares

Extra space for extra practice.

Beijing

The thriving capital city of China is home to beautiful palaces and a hundred-acre city square. Around Beijing, you can see…

kàn
to see

Picture it

看 kàn ("to see") includes a hand above an eye, as though shielding your eyes from the sun.

How to write it:

Your turn:

长城

Chángchéng

The Great Wall

Your turn:

故宫

Gùgōng

The Forbidden City

Your turn:

天安门广场

Tiān'ānmén Guǎngchǎng

Tiananmen Square

Your turn:

A day in the country

China is not all big cities. It also has a beautiful and varied countryside.

First learn the characters for morning and afternoon.

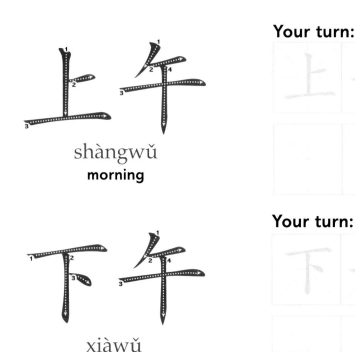

shàngwǔ
morning

Your turn:

xiàwǔ
afternoon

Your turn:

Picture it
This might help you remember the characters.

above
shàng
上 + 午 = **morning**

下 + 午 = **afternoon**

xià
under

wǔ
midday

Plan your day

Now say what you are going to do in the morning and afternoon.

Write the characters in the boxes.

Morning 上午

Your turn:

páshān

climb a mountain

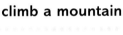

Afternoon 下午

Your turn:

zuò chuán

take a boat ride

Your turn:

qí mǎ

ride a horse

Useful phrases

These phrases will help you get by in China.

Qǐng nǐ zài shuō.

Please can you say it again.
(pronounced "ching knee z-eye sh-war")

Your turn:

你说英文吗?

Nǐ shuō yīngwén ma?

Do you speak English?

Your turn:

你	说	英	文	吗	？

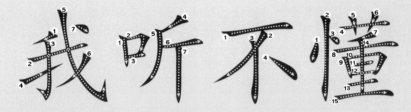

我听不懂

Wǒ tīng bù dǒng.

I don't understand.

Your turn:

我	听	不	懂

Shopping list

Need some souvenirs? Time to go shopping!

pǐn

thing / article

Picture it

The character shows three containers. Draw some things you would like to buy in the boxes.

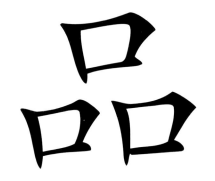

Getting the stroke order right for boxes is useful because they often appear in Chinese characters.

How to write it:

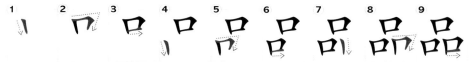

Your turn:

Here are some things you might buy:

Your turn:

sīzhīpǐn

silk
(pronounced "suh-juh-pin")

Your turn:

jìniànpǐn

souvenirs
(pronounced "jee-nee-en-pin")

Your turn:

gōngyìpǐn

crafts

Festival!

If you are in China in late January or early February, you might be lucky and catch Chinese New Year.

If so, you will definitely find this phrase useful to know.

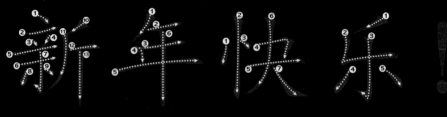

Xīnnián kuàilè!

Happy New Year!

Your turn:

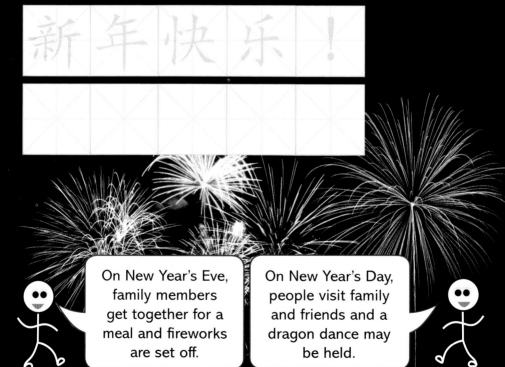

On New Year's Eve, family members get together for a meal and fireworks are set off.

On New Year's Day, people visit family and friends and a dragon dance may be held.

Let's party!

There are other major festivals in China.

Zhōng qiū jié

Mid-Autumn Festival

Your turn:

Duān wǔ jié

Dragon Boat Festival

Your turn:

Wherever you go, and whatever you do in China, have fun learning Mandarin Chinese!

Character practice 10

Practice the characters from this section here.

坐船

骑马

请你再说

你说英文吗？

我听不懂

品

More to do!

Keep going. This section includes these characters, too.

丝织品

纪念品

工艺品

新年快乐！

中秋节

端午节

Practice squares

Extra space for extra practice.

Certificate

Congratulations to:

....

for successfully finishing this book.

好哇,干得漂亮!

Hǎo wa, gànde piàoliang!

Bravo! Well done!

Remember the golden rules of writing: If in doubt, write top to bottom, left to right!

Date:

....

Pronunciation guide

Pinyin is like a language all its own. Use this rough guide to help you pronounce the words in this book.

Initial	Sound
b	baw
p	paw
m	maw
f	faw
d	duh
t	tuh
n	nuh
l	luh
g	guh
k	kuh
h	huh
j	gee

Initial	Sound
q	chee
x	she
z	dzuh
c	tsuh
s	suh
zh	jir
ch	chir
sh	shir
r	rj
w	ooh
y	ee

Final	Sound
a	ah
ai	i
ao	ow
an	ahn
ang	ahng
o	aw
ong	oong
ou	oh
e	uh
ei	ay
en	un
eng	ung

Final	Sound
er	ar
i	ee/uh
ia	ya
iao	yaow
ian	yan
iang	yahng
ie	yeh
in	een
ing	eeng
iong	yoong
iu	you
u	oo

Final	Sound
ua	wa
uo	waw
ui	way
uai	why
uan	won
un	un
uang	wahng
ü	yoo
ue	oo-weh
üan	ywan
ün	ywen

Useful words

Use this alphabetical list of words from the book for quick reference.

afternoon	xiàwǔ	下午
at	zài	在
autumn	qiūtiān	秋天
ball	qiú	球
basketball	lánqiú	篮球
bicycle	zìxíngchē	自行车
big	dà	大
birthday	shēngrì	生日
brother (older)	gēge	哥哥
brother (younger)	dìdi	弟弟
to buy	mǎi	买
car	qìchē	汽车
chicken	jī	鸡
China	Zhōngguó	中国
Chinese person	Zhōngguórén	中国人
chopsticks	kuàizi	筷子
cold	lěng	冷

dim sum	diǎnxīn	点心
to drink	hē	喝
east	dōng	东
to eat	chī	吃
to enter	jìn	进
father	bàba	爸爸
fish	yú	鱼
fruit	shuǐguǒ	水果
to go	qù	去
good-bye	zàijiàn	再见
hello	nǐ hǎo	你好
hot	rè	热
I	wǒ	我
knife	dāo	刀
to like	xǐhuan	喜欢
to love	ài	爱
man	nánrén	男人
menu	càidān	菜单
moon	yuè	月
morning	shàngwǔ	上午

mother	māma	妈妈
no / not	bù	不
noodles	miàntiáo	面条
north	běi	北
to paint	huàhuà	画画
person	rén	人
please	qǐng	请
rain	yǔ	雨
restaurant	fàndiàn	饭店
restroom	cèsuǒ	厕所
rice	mǐfàn	米饭
to see	kàn	看
silk	sīzhīpǐn	丝织品
sister (older)	jiějie	姐姐
sister (younger)	mèimei	妹妹
to sit	zuò	坐
small	xiǎo	小
soccer	zúqiú	足球
south	nán	南
souvenir	jìniànpǐn	纪念品

spoon	sháozi	勺子
spring	chūntiān	春天
to study	xuéxí	学习
summer	xiàtiān	夏天
table tennis	pīngpāngqiú	乒乓球
tea	chá	茶
tennis	wǎngqiú	网球
thank you	xièxie	谢谢
thing / article	pǐn	品
ticket	piào	票
train	huǒchē	火车
vehicle	chē	车
waiter	fúwùyuán	服务员
to want	xiǎng	想
west	xī	西
where	nǎr	哪儿
which	nǎ gè	哪个
winter	dōngtiān	冬天
woman	nǚrén	女人
you	nǐ	你

Answers

p.19 1) zàijiàn **2)** xièxie **3)** nǐhǎo
p.23 1) Fàndiàn zài nǎr? **2)** Shūdiàn zài nǎr?
3) Cháguǎn zài nǎr? **4)** Cèsuǒ zài nǎr?
p.26 1) 请进 **2)** 请坐 **3)** 请喝茶
p. 38-39 1) 小 **2)** 大 **3)** 大 **4)** 小
p.43 Zhè shì wǒ de māma.
p.53 Geography test 1) Jiānádà **2)** Yīngguó
3) Hélán **4)** Měiguó **5)** Fǎguó **6)** Zhōngguó
Your turn 1) Nǐ shì nǎ guó rén?

2) Wǒ shì Měiguórén. **3)** Wǒ shì Fǎguórén.
4) Wǒ shì Rìběnrén.
p.58 1) 15 **2)** 40 **3)** 18 **4)** 14 **5)** 23 **6)** 71 **7)** 99 **8)** 58
p.59 1) 230 **2)** 60,000 **3)** 4,300 **4)** 90,000
p. 81 1) yòubiān 1 zuǒbiān 2
2) yìzhízǒu 1 yòubiān 2 zuǒbiān 3
p.83 2) wǔ diǎn **3)** jiǔ diǎn bàn **4)** èr diǎn èrshí fēn
p.95 Literally: "Waiter, I want to eat dim sum." but a
better translation is: "Waiter, I'd like some dim sum."

About the author

Elinor Greenwood graduated from Leeds University with a degree in Modern Chinese Studies. She has lived and worked in China for many years. She presently lives near Cambridge, UK, and divides her time between writing language books and teaching children Mandarin. She is the author of *Get Talking Chinese* and *Fun and Easy Chinese*.

Please see her website for more information:
www.noodlepublishing.com

Picture credits

The publisher would like to thank the following for their kind permission to reproduce their photographs:
(Key: a-above; b-below/bottom; c-center; f-far; l-left; r-right; t-top)

3 Dreamstime.com: Stockyimages. **11 Corbis:** Frederic Soltan / Terra. **23 Corbis:** Claro Cortes IV / Reuters (crb); Tim Graham / Encyclopedia (cr); Imaginechina / Corbis Wire (clb). **29 Corbis:** John Lund / Sam Diephuis / Blend Images. **35 Dreamstime.com:** Szefei. **37 Dreamstime.com:** Szefei. **38 Dorling Kindersley:** Tim Draper / Rough Guides (br); University of Pennsylvania Museum of Archaeology and Anthropology (bl). **39 Fotolia:** Eric Isselee (bl). **43 Alamy Images:** Erik Isakson / RubberBall. **64 Corbis:** Simon Marcus / Flame. **70 Dreamstime.com:** Hurry (bl); Yong hian Lim / Jojojojo (cl). **71 Dreamstime.com:** Sean Pavone / Sepavo. (bl).

Getty Images: aaaaimages / Moment Open (cla). **73 Dreamstime.com:** Chuyu (cl); Lee Snider / Leesniderphotoimages (tl); Shannon Fagan / Xixinxing (tr); Herman118 (cr). **92 Corbis:** 13 / Image Source / Ocean. **95 Corbis:** Foodfolio / Food and Drink Photos / Canopy (tl). **104 Dorling Kindersley:** Stephen Oliver (fcra). **Getty Images:** Photographer's Choice RF / Burazin (cra). **111 Corbis:** Ann Purcell,Carl (b); Yang Liu / Terra (cl). **Dorling Kindersley:** Tim Draper / Rough Guides (tl). **113 Corbis:** T. J. Kirkpatrick / Corbis News (bl); Keith Levit / Design Pics / Canopy (cl). **114 Dorling Kindersley:** Tim Draper / Rough Guides. **117 Dorling Kindersley:** Sarah Ashun (bl). **118 Fotolia:** Sherri Camp. **119 Dreamstime.com:** Mike K. / Mikekwok (cr); Erica Schroeder / Stelya (bl). **Getty Images:** ChinaFotoPress (cra).

All other images © Dorling Kindersley
For further information see: www.dkimages.com